Animal Habitats

Rainforest Habitats

Written by Noah Leatherland

KidHaven Publishing

Published in 2025 by
KidHaven Publishing, an Imprint of
Greenhaven Publishing, LLC
2544 Clinton St., Buffalo, NY 14224

Written by: Noah Leatherland
Edited by: Elise Carraway
Designed by: Amy Li

Cataloging-in-Publication Data

Names: Leatherland, Noah, 1999-.
Title: Rainforest habitats / Noah Leatherland.
Description: Buffalo, NY : KidHaven Publishing, 2025. | Series: Animal habitats | Includes glossary and index.
Identifiers: ISBN 9781534548275 (pbk.) | ISBN 9781534548282 (library bound) | ISBN 9781534548299 (ebook)
Subjects: LCSH: Rain forest animals--Juvenile literature. | Rain forests--Juvenile literature.
Classification: LCC QL112.L43 2025 | DDC 591.734--dc2

Manufactured in the United States of America

CPSIA compliance information: Batch #CSKH25
For further information contact Greenhaven Publishing LLC at 1-844-317-7404.

Please visit our website, www.greenhavenpublishing.com.
For a free color catalog of all our high-quality books, call toll free 1-844-317-7404 or fax 1-844-317-7405.

Find us on

Photo Credits. Images are courtesy of Shutterstock.com. With thanks to Getty Images, Thinkstock Photo and iStockphoto.
Recurring – MirabellePrint, Macrovector. Cover – Macrovector, Hung Chung Chih, GUDKOV ANDREY, KittyVector, dangdumrong. 2–3 – SJ Travel Photo and Video. 4–5 – AustralianCamera, Nicola_K_photos. 6–7 – CherylRamalho, kotoffei, neelsky. 8–9 – Enrico Pescantini, M Gustafson Photography. 10–11 – Tim Fleming, Xico Putini. 12–13 – GUDKOV ANDREY, juan Francisco valbuena, MVshop, tiverylucky. 14–15 – Alamin-Khan, Linas T, Nemanja Cosovic, Stephen Clarke. 16–17 – Abdul Fattah19, Nickolas warner, Petr Muckstein. 18–19 – Jan Hejda, Karel Bartik. 20–21 – Alves-Silva K. R, curiosity, Vaclav Sebek. 22–23 – AustralianCamera, EcoPrint, Lili Kudrili.

Contents

Words that look like <u>this</u> can be found in the glossary on page 24.

What Is a Habitat?

A habitat is where a living thing makes its home. There is everything a living thing needs in its habitat, such as food, water, and shelter. Animals have different ways of surviving in their habitat.

animals in a grassland habitat

Rainforests

Rainforests are forests with lots of trees that get a lot of rainfall. There are a few layers in rainforests. There are many amazing animals that live in each layer of the rainforest.

Bengal Tiger

Bengal tigers are top predators in their rainforest habitats. Their stripes help them blend into the bushes, grasses, and trees. This helps them stay hidden from their prey.

Many Bengal tigers live in the rainforests of Asia.

When a Bengal tiger catches its prey, it might not eat it all right away. Bengal tigers use bushes in the rainforest to hide their food so that they can come back to it later.

Sloth

Sloths are found in South and Central America.

Sloths are known for being very slow animals. Surprisingly, this helps them to survive in the rainforest. Moving slowly means that sloths are less likely to be spotted by predators.

Being slow also helps sloths hide in other ways. Algae grows on sloths' fur because they do not move much. This makes their fur look green and keeps them hidden in the trees.

Toco Toucan

The toco toucan is the biggest type of toucan. They have very long bills. Their bills help them keep their bodies cool in the warm rainforests they live in.

Toco toucans live in South America.

Toucans hop between branches because they are not good at flying.

The toucan's long bill helps it reach for food. Toucans grab fruit from the rainforest's trees and sometimes take food from other birds' nests. They can even peel fruit with their bills!

Ring-Tailed Lemur

Ring-tailed lemurs spend a lot of time on the ground as well as climbing through the rainforest's trees. Their fingers and toes help them grab onto branches. Their tails help them balance.

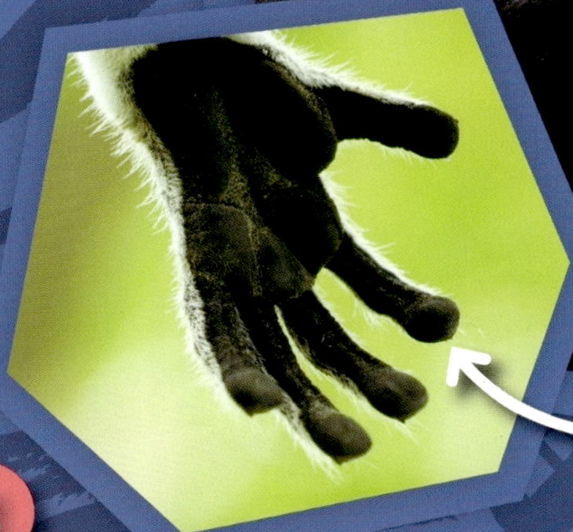

a lemur's fingers

Lemurs have strong legs that make them very good at jumping. They can leap from tree to tree and move through the rainforest much quicker than running along the forest floor.

Lemurs are only found in Madagascar.

Red-Eyed Tree Frog

Red-eyed tree frogs live in the trees. They have suckers on their feet that cling onto leaves. They lay their eggs on the leaves above ponds. Then, their young fall in when they hatch.

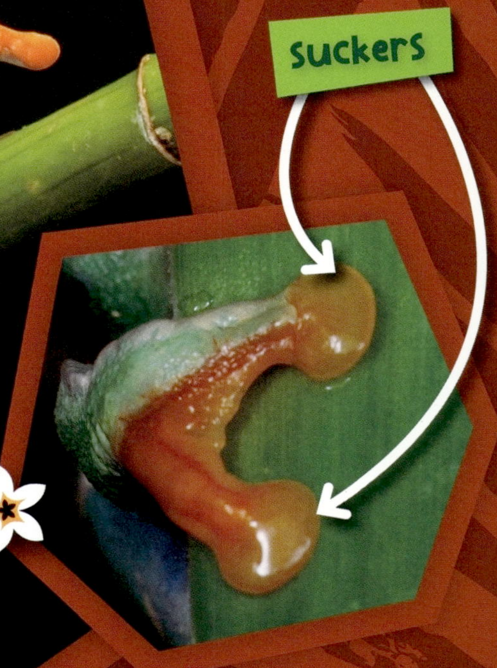

Red-eyed tree frogs are found in Central and South America.

Red-eyed tree frogs use their colors to distract predators. Before a predator can attack, they open their bright eyes wide. The flash of color surprises the predator so that the frog can get away.

Goliath Beetle

Goliath beetles are found in African rainforests.

Goliath beetles are tough insects that are well suited to survive in the rainforest. They have a strong exoskeleton that protects them. They can also lift things over 800 times heavier than themselves.

Goliath beetles eat sugary things such as tree sap and fruits. They have very strong jaws that can bite through tough plants and the bark of rainforest trees.

Boa Constrictor

The color and pattern of a boa constrictor's scales help them blend in with the rainforest's plants. This lets them sneak up on their prey. They wrap their bodies around their prey and squeeze.

Boa constrictors are found in Central and South America.

Bushes, leaves, and trees can get in the way of a boa constrictor's <u>vision</u>. Instead of finding prey by sight, they use other <u>senses</u>. These snakes can smell their prey and feel the prey's body heat.

Boa constrictors use their tongues to find smells.

Harpy Eagle

Harpy eagles are strong enough to grab their prey from out of trees. They have shorter wings than other eagles. These shorter wings help them fly between branches in the rainforest.

Harpy eagles build their nests in the highest trees of the rainforest. This helps them keep their chicks safe from other rainforest predators. A high nest also lets them look out for prey.

Harpy eagles live in Central and South America.

Animal Habitats

Lots of animals can be found in every part of the rainforest. They might live high in the trees or down low on the ground. They are all important in keeping the rainforest <u>ecosystem</u> healthy.

There are many beautiful habitats around the world. Each one is important. Taking care of these habitats helps the wonderful creatures that live in them survive.

Glossary

algae	a plantlike living thing that has no roots, stems, leaves, or flowers
bill	another name for the beak of some types of birds
ecosystem	a community of living things and the environment they live in
exoskeleton	the hard structure on the outside of some animals
hatch	to come out of an egg
predator	an animal that hunts other animals for food
prey	an animal that is hunted by other animals for food
sap	a sticky liquid found inside trees and other plants
senses	the ways an animal takes in information about their surroundings, including hearing, sight, and touch
vision	sight

Index